JOURN__ _
YOUR SOUL PURPOSE

GUIDED WORKBOOK

Vayia Nafees

ISBN-13: 978-1976358050
ISBN-10: 1976358051

Published in Great Britain in October 2017 by:
Vayia Nafees - Be Your Spirit
www.beyourspirit.co.uk

TESTIMONIALS

"I have known Vayia for a couple of years now. Initially this was for Reiki when I was going through a period of illness, but I have continued to see her for well I suppose you could call it emotional support and she has become a friend now.

My friendship with Vayia is a very important to me. It seems we found each other at the right time – the universe was listening I think. She is supportive and incredibly intuitive, often blowing my mind with her insight into how I could look differently at things to see the answers more clearly.

She told me that my purpose was my passion and that if I let that thought settle then the answers I was searching for would come, and they did.

As a friend she is funny, caring, intelligent and in tune to her environment. She has been through enough of life to understand how things work and has a lot to offer. You feel instantly relaxed in her presence, when she gives you a hug it is always full of love. If I had to pick one word to describe her it would be Genuine.

Her new book is a collaboration of years of learning and practising what she preaches. She does believe we can all be the best we can and simply loves to enable us to achieve the goals we set for ourselves.

Thank you Vayia for being you and thank you for being my friend."

Kate Collier, Maidenhead (UK)

" I have worked with Vayia for a number of years and I can honestly say I wouldn't be the person I am today without her. She has an incredible talent for understanding the deeper self and helping you work towards overcoming your emotional blockages and obstacles. She is an extraordinary therapist who's boundless passion for helping others is at the core of every thing she does.

The guided workbook is a blessing to anyone who reads it. It enables one to give space, time and thought to understanding and fulling their purpose. With amazing questions and meditations, Vayia's book can open you up to whole different level and outlook.

I thoroughly recommend Vayia's book, 'Journey to your soul purpose' to every individual to bring more happiness and contentment into their life."

Fiona Jones, Brighton (UK)

be your spirit

*I would like to dedicate my book to my wonderful
teachers that were so open and kind to share all their
knowledge and experience with me and to my family
for their constant love and support.*

Vayia Nafees

CONTENTS

Are you ready to fulfil your life purpose? **Are you bored of doing a job you dislike?** Would you like to spend your days doing something fulfilling that also brings you income? Do you want more meaning in your life?

This journal is designed to help you discover for yourself your true calling in this life. Remember this is a vast and ever-changing subject; purpose is not necessarily one thing. Rather it is about living from your heart: if you follow the guidance from your heart you are then automatically fulfilling your life purpose every single day.

Your purpose is not just a thing that you love doing. It also gives meaning to your life. How can we interpret the word 'meaning'? Everyone experiences this in a unique way; being present and aware as you navigate towards a more fulfilling life will allow you to feel 'meaning' in your life as it begins to bubble up.

The key is to follow your heart and intuition, not your mind. This is contrary to everything we've been taught to do. Western culture teaches us 'Mind over Matter': think with your brains, logic and intellect instead of your heart. Deep down inside of you, you know exactly what you love doing! But due to our busy western world lives and the education and societal pressures we grew up with, this knowledge was buried.

This knowledge is now ready to be unleashed. It is time to remove barriers from the mind, go deep within and find the truth that lives within yourself.

Within this journal you will find different tips, hints, clues, exercises and questions that will help you to find the answers you are looking for. If you follow this writing journal you will find your purpose/passions/loves and dreams. I hope you enjoy this time and present that you are giving to yourself, this is already the first step and actually the only step, this is why I know you will find and fulfil your purpose because you have already bought this guided workbook, so have faith things will start to change rather quickly, or as quickly as you take this time to reflect.

Wouldn't it be amazing if you live everyday with so much enthusiasm and excitement that you feel like the luckiest person alive? Remember, your life is valuable, so please don't spend anytime wasting it. You only remember one life. One day it will end (hopefully later rather than sooner); carry this awareness with you to give you the energy and motivation to create your best life. It is time to begin living the life you so deserve and want to live.

Fulfil your Purpose

I invite you on a journey of self-discovery, passion and awakening and I very much wish you all the love, support and action needed to complete your destiny.

Even though it may feel like it, it's really not that hard. Just follow my guide and watch the wonderful changes in your life happen. I thank you for letting me give you this gift, as you enable me to fulfil my life purpose.

Much love and happiness,
Vayia x

Remembering What You Love

First, we need to find out what you love doing. Believe it or not, your life purpose will be something that you love to do; how magical is that!

Deep down, we all know what our calling is and what we want to accomplish in this lifetime. Therefore all we need to do is go inside and listen.

So find a quiet space, make a tea or coffee, and start to write 10 things you love doing.

1

2

3

4

5

6

7

8

9

10

If you can't think of them all now, don't worry.
Just take some time over the next couple of days
to think about what else you love.

When you have thought of 10 things you love doing you
are ready to move on to the next
questions below:

How many times per day do you do the things you love?

How many times per week do you do the things you love?

Would you like to do something you love everyday?

CHAPTER 2

Going Deeper

We live in a western society that is busy and often stressful. Being able to listen to what our heart truly wants is usually quite difficult as there is too much outside and inside noise. What we truly desire comes from our heart, not our mind. Our mind has been subjected to different thoughts and teachings our whole life. Our minds have been influenced by society, schooling, situations, experiences, our parents, and much more. There is nothing to blame here, but the point is: What your mind might say you want is most probably not what your heart says you want.

The key is by listening, making decisions and acting from the information you receive from your heart: you will then live your purpose, hear your intuition and find more happiness and joy in your every day life.

The next part of this journal is really important. It is about implementing changes into your life that will quiet your mind so it is actually possible to hear your heart. Your heart will never shout over your mind, like the mind does over the heart. Your heart will only whisper to you therefore it is really important that we will take the next couple of weeks calming the mind so you are able to hear your hearts true desires.

One of the easiest and a very effective way to slow the mind down are breathing exercises. The slower and more concentrated the breathing you do the more the mind has no choice but to also become slower and more focused

'The more your mind calms down and the more you reconnect with your body, the more you will be able to hear your intuition and understand what your heart says.'

Please go to YouTube and type Vayia Nafees in the search bar and click on the video Yogic Breathing. This video will take 15 minutes to complete. Please take a minute to notice how your mind is before taking part in the breathing exercises and how your mind feels after.

I hope you enjoyed the breathing exercises and feel a bit more calm and centered. The breathing exercises are a really easy and efficient way that you can start to come out of your mind and reconnect with your body.

Your next task is to implement these breathing exercises into your daily life. Practice one round of all the breathing exercises everyday. It will only take you 15 minutes per day for the next 2 weeks, and you will start to notice your mind is calmer, giving you more space to feel and hear messages from within.

I .... promise to do the breathing exercises every day for the next two weeks so I will be able to connect with my inner guidance.

CHAPTER 3

Dreaming BIG

It's time to start thinking BIG.

I want you to start imagining everything you want to BE, DO and HAVE in life.

So let's break this down:

What do you want to DO in your lifetime?

What do you want to HAVE in your life?

This is where you write **the bucket list**.
Write down everything you want
to do before you die.

Now with your bucket list prioritise the list so put the most important ones first.

1

2

3

4

5

6

7

8

9

10

WHAT DO YOU WANT TO BE IN THIS LIFE?
(Apart from your loving gorgeous self)

1

2

3

4

5

6

7

8

9

10

Dreaming BIG!

Take some time everyday to keep daydreaming. Try to daydream and imagine all the time, starting by imagining what you would like to do every day, month, or year.

- **Do you want to travel more?**
- **Do you want to go out for dinners more?**
- **Do you need help at home?**
- **Do you want to coach others?**
- **Do you want to design your own clothes or your own furniture?**
- **Do you want to write books?**
- **Do you want to write songs?**
- **Do you want to play music?**
- **Do you want to dance?**
- **Do you want to teach?**
- **Do you want to travel the world and document something that is close to your heart?**
- **Do you want to make a documentary for the world to see?**
- **Do you want to own a successful business that sells something you love?**
- **Do you want to be the leading lady in your field?**

These are just some examples to get your imagination started. From now on, let yourself daydream of what you would love to do, or what you would love your life to look like.

Now write all your ideas and dreams in the dream bubbles provided.

Write down 10 things you love about yourself:

1

2

3

4

5

6

7

8

9

10

CHAPTER 4

Opening The Mind

The bigger you start dreaming, the more your mind may start to say, "Well, you can't do that because of this" or "you can't do that because you won't make enough money" or "you're not capable of that". The list is endless. We call these LIMITING BELIEFS. They are limiting what you could be doing, they are limiting you being the best person you can be and accomplishing what you are here to accomplish.

Opening the Mind

I want you to make a promise that for the whole time it takes you to work through this writing journal, you will not give these limiting beliefs any energy. Yes, they might come up, but I want you to notice them and I want you to tell your mind, "I don't care what you think right now because maybe there is a way." Your mind will try to tell you there is not, or answer you in a different way. Just ignore the answer.

I .... promise not to give any limiting beliefs any energy every day while working through this journal.

I also want you to start practising sentences that start with

"**How** and **What**".

For example:

1. **How** come that doing what I love to do will make me a fortune?
2. **How** come I get to do what I love to do every day?
3. **How** come I get to choose when I work?
4. **How** come I am the luckiest person in the world?

and

1. **What** if I really could do what I always wanted to do?
2. **What** if I really could have that business I have always wanted?
3. **What** if I really could write the book I always wanted to write?
   Or paint the pictures I always wanted to paint?
4. **What** if I really could travel the world?

When you practice the '**How**' and '**What**' sentences, never listen to the answers. These sentences just start to open your mind to more possibilities, which is very important for this process.

Again, please don't listen to the answers. The point here is just to let your mind expand. It is to get your mind on your side rather than against you.

Dreams

Little ideas will get you little results. If you think big ideas, big thoughts, and extreme success, then this is what you will get.

'Reach for the moon, even if you fall short you will land among the stars.'

Write down five dreams you have that you wish to accomplish before you die. They could be long-lost dreams that you have forgotten about. Take as much time as you need to come up with **five amazing dreams**. Dreams wherein if you actually accomplished them then you know you have given your life your very best shot.

Dreams

Dreams

Dreams

5

Releasing The Old

What do you NOT love that you don't want to do anymore? (There is always something that we can drop from our lives that does not serve us anymore. We need to drop something to make room for the new things that we love doing). Think hard and write down one or more things you don't want in your life anymore. These can be anything from a job, to a person, to a past experience/situation, even a food or a habit that you'd like to be free of. Just something that actually depletes your energy rather than gives you energy.

What do you not love?

Once you have decided at least one thing you would like to let go of from your life then find a comfy spot and then please go to YouTube and type Vayia Nafees into the search bar and click on the video titled: 'Releasing The Old.' With this 10 minute guided meditation I will ask for anything that is not serving you anymore to be released so you can make room for new wonderful opportunities and people to come into your life. Don't worry if you've never done meditation before; all you will do is lie down, relax, and go with the flow.

I have left space below for you to write notes about whatever came up during the meditation if you feel so inclined.

Notes on Meditation cont.

6

Going Even Deeper

MAKE MORE SPACE IN YOUR LIFE FOR YOU

Now it is time to go a bit deeper. As mentioned before the only way for you to be able to really listen to your heart and follow the advice your heart will give is by calming your mind and getting in touch with your body.

If you are super busy in your life you will not have the time you need to be able to reflect and listen to what your heart and body are saying. You have to create time in your life for you. **To do activities you love and also just to sit, write, reflect, and listen to your inner guidance.** This is the only way you will work out your life purpose.

So you need to free up time for you. Have a think and write down some things below that you can stop doing in order to have more time. It is important that you reflect on where you spend your energy and decide what things you do that actually you don't need to be doing anymore, therefore creating more time for you.

1

2

3

4

5

I also want to talk about prioritising yourself. Some of us grew up with the understanding that everything we should be doing is for others; for your family, for your school, for your company, for your community, for your country. However, what about **for you**? If you are looking after everyone else, who is looking after you?

YOU are the only one that can look after yourself, so don't feel selfish or guilty saying no to people, situations, or things in order to give yourself more time, space, and energy. If you give this time to yourself and do what you love to do you will be able to give unconditional love and energy to others in the future.

If you keep giving and giving to others and not to yourself, you will eventually burn out and you will not be able to give anything to anyone- not even yourself. That's just how it works, you will be completely drained because you did not look after yourself. Again, this is your choice: start to free up your time so you can spend this time on you. You are allowed to make this choice; but further to that, the people who love you WANT you to do this. They don't want a door mat or a slave, and they don't want to see someone they love burn themselves out. They want to see the person they love achieving their dreams and passions. Begin putting your own needs first and you will notice that not only will you gain more love and energy from the people around you but you will also inspire others, they will learn from your actions and they will start to take care of themselves.

Once you understand how important it is to bring a balance into your life, you will actually be able to start living your purpose. Eastern cultures understand this balance thing very well, however we in Western societies are far away from achieving balance.

Most of the activities we do all day are Yang activities; these types of activities are more active, strong, busy activities. The Yang energy is our fiery energy; it is the energy behind all the action you take to get things done.

Whereas Yin energy (the energy most of us in the western world are lacking) is the restorative energy; this energy allows our mind and body to slow down and rest and relax.

This is the energy that you have to bring back into your life if you really want to fulfil your life purpose: if you really want to follow your hearts desires, if you really want to live a happy and balanced life, if you really want to be in touch with your intuition and see the big picture in life, if you really want to dream big, make a difference or truly succeed, then this is the energy you are going to have to cultivate.

Within the next 2 weeks you are going to cultivate this Yin energy into your life.

If we are moving too quickly, please take a break to digest what we have already gone through. This can be a good thing. If you need to take a break to process or make the changes needed to create space in your life, then please do so and come back to this point when you are ready.

TAKE TIME
TO DO WHAT
MAKES YOUR
SOUL HAPPY.

I will give you a list of Yin activities you can implement in your everyday life that will help you calm your mind and reconnect with your body. The more energy and time you put into this venture the more you will get out of it.

If you already go to yoga, change your yoga class to a yin yoga session. If you don't go to yoga, then try a class: it may surprise you. Yoga has so many benefits, and if you can seek out a yin yoga class you will bring the Yin energy into your life. If you can bring that energy into your life, then you can calm your mind, and you will be able to hear your heart and recognise your inner guidance and wisdom.

The Yin energy is the energy from the moon; even going to bed early (like 10 p.m.) will help you to receive the yin energy. Staying in a couple of evenings a week to listen to relaxing music and do this workbook will also bring some Yin energy into your life.

Meditation has some amazing benefits and works very well in calming the mind. The word meditation may put you off, or you may relate very well. Meditation is simply focus and concentration, so any activity you like doing that brings focus and concentration will help your mind to be in the present moment. For example: painting, washing up, making things, and so on.

This is also why it is important that you continue to do your breathing exercises every day. They bring the restorative energy to your mind and body. The next page is a promise page. This promise is really important for you to achieve your dreams and success. It is a promise to yourself that you will implement at least four Yin activities a week for the next couple of weeks. The promise also includes doing these breathing exercises every day for the next 2 weeks. As mentioned before, this is the way to get in touch with your wisdom, inner guidance, dreams, and wishes.

The last part of the promise is that you take the time to listen to your intuition, dreams and conversations over the next couple of weeks as these are all signs regarding your life purpose. Carry around a little notebook so you remember to jot them down before you forget them.

Activities you can choose from:

1. Please go to YouTube and type Vayia Nafees in the search bar and listen to the video titled: 'Reconnect to Your Body Guided Meditation'.

2. Yin Yoga class

3. Going to bed before 10 p.m.

4. Spending the evening at home alone; you may listen to relaxing music and write, however, no TV, no talking on the phone, and no posting on the internet

5. Painting/drawing/writing

6. Spending time at home cooking yourself a delicious healthy meal and eating on your own

7. Having a bath

8. Go for a massage

9. Go for an acupuncture session

10. Go for a Reiki treatment

11. Go for a walk in the nature (not running)

12. Something you LOVE doing

13. Dancing by yourself at home

14. Meditation

I hope you enjoy the next two weeks of spending some time on yourself. On the next page you will find the Sacred Promise page; please complete this. After the promise page you will find two weekly sheets. Every time you complete a Yin activity, you can add it to the weekly sheet. The minimum requirement is four Yin activities per week; however, the more you can implement the better. Please remember to take notes of any emotions, dreams, intuitions and signs that you notice. Write down as much as you can within the next two weeks.

SACRED PROMISE

I .... promise to complete the 4 breathing exercises every day for the next 2 weeks.

I .... promise to add a minimum of four activities each week for the next two weeks including listening to the guided meditation (titled Reconnect to Your Body).

I .... promise to be open to understanding my life purpose by listening to my intuition, remembering and writing down my dreams, and watching out for signs from the universe through conversations, people, and situations.

1st Week Activity Log

DAY	Activity 1	Activity 2	Activity 3	Activity 4
MONDAY				
TUESDAY				
WEDNESDAY				
THURSDAY				
FRIDAY				
SATURDAY				
SUNDAY				

2nd Week Activity Log

DAY	Activity 1	Activity 2	Activity 3	Activity 4
MONDAY				
TUESDAY				
WEDNESDAY				
THURSDAY				
FRIDAY				
SATURDAY				
SUNDAY				

Welcome Back

SECOND
SECTION (ONLY
TO BE LOOKED
AT ONCE
YOU HAVE
COMPLETED
THE LAST TWO
WEEKS)

Welcome back! I really hope you had a lovely and inspiring two weeks and you received lots of messages, hints, and ideas towards your life purpose. You should also feel a bit more balanced and rejuvenated. If you do not feel that balance, then I would say that you are very disconnected from your body, which is common in the western world due to the business of our lives, and in turn our minds. However, do not give up! It just means the path to understanding is longer for you. Luckily, the enjoyment comes from the journey and not the destination, so take as long as you need to understand what it is that you truly want. Carry on with implementing Yin activities into your everyday life and slowly make the changes needed in your life in order to become more connected with your body and higher self. If you have a good idea about your purpose for the time being, then let's carry on through this workbook.

I hope you enjoyed spending time with yourself the last two weeks. I hope you feel more energised from the breathing exercises and more clear with what you want to be doing at this point in your life. I am also assuming that your life has started to change a little as you have let go of things that are not serving you and you are spending more time on yourself.

Even if right now you do not have the complete under-standing of what your life purpose is, it does not ac-tually matter. What matters is that you can hear what your heart wants; if you can hear your heart, follow her guidance. That is your path and that will lead you to your life purpose. As you move along this path, your purpose will become clearer, and there is no longer any need to be rigid about your dreams. The further you go, the more you accomplish, and the bigger and more ever-changing your dreams will become. This is very normal once you live your dream: more big dreams will be realised.

Hear what your Heart wants.

What you want to do

Please write below what is it you want to do. There can be more than one. I will give you an example of mine. I wanted to be a Reiki Teacher, Yoga Teacher and an International Best Seller. It was as simple as that; this is what I wanted to do before I died, so this is what I wrote down. Please write what you want to do and what you want to accomplish before you die. This is exactly what you are going to work towards.

1

2

3

4

5

8

CHAPTER

Releasing Your Limiting Beliefs

If you have any limiting beliefs (which we talked about on page three) that are telling you that you will not be able to achieve any of your desires above, then please follow the instructions below.

It's important you are in a quiet space with no disturbances for this session, so do what you need to do. Shut the door or turn off the phone, do whatever it takes so you can be undisturbed for the next 20 minutes.

Releasing your limiting beliefs

First I want you to start with the four breathing exercises to get you into a calm zone, so please do those now.

Once you've completed the breathing exercises I want you to look at your first desire above and ask yourself: can you achieve this? If the answer is yes, then skip this section. If your mind is telling you that you cannot complete this, then please write down exactly what the mind is telling you. For example, "You will never succeed. You can't do this as it will not bring you enough money. You can't do this as it does not exist. You can't do this because you are not good enough", and so on.

Please write your Limiting Belief below:

....

....

Please ask yourself again if there is any other reason you would not be able to succeed in your first desire:

....

....

And then ask one more time (sometimes we have no limiting beliefs, and sometimes we have many). It is just what our mind has grasped onto from past experiences and situations.

....

....

As you look above you can clearly read the beliefs that are holding you back from achieving your dreams.

What if these beliefs aren't actually true?
What if your mind got it wrong?
What if you could truly succeed in what you want?

Once you are aware of these beliefs, you don't actually have to believe them anymore. You can let them go. They are just beliefs. They are not facts.

Remember the section earlier about starting your sentences with '**How** and **What**'? I want you to do this is now. We are going to play with your limiting belief. I will give you an example below:

Limiting Belief: It is not possible to make money doing what I love.

Then you would write:

1. **How** it is possible that I can make money from doing what I absolutely love?

2. **What** if it was possible to make money doing what I absolutely love?

Releasing your limiting beliefs

Please write your limiting belief below and then write the 'How' and 'What' sentences to go with it. (Remember, don't listen to the answer your mind throws back, it's just about repeating these 'How' and 'What' sentences over and over. The more times the better.)

LIMITING BELIEF 1

....

....

1. **How**

....

....

2. **What**

....

....

LIMITING BELIEF 2

....

....

1. **How**

....

....

2. **What**

....

....

....

....

1. **How**

....

....

2. **What**

....

....

51

Ask for Help!

Now we are going to ask for help. You can ask for help from whoever or whatever you believe in; whether it is God or Angels, Mother Earth, Humanity or Yourself, it really does not matter what you believe! But do know it is important to believe in something. If you don't believe in anything, you cling on to things and relationships so tightly with so much fear that you will never know how to live in faith, trust, hope, joy, and love. Have a think about this. Do you have Faith that things will work out? Do you have Trust that you will be fine and you will accomplish what you want in life? Do you Hope for more? For a better future? And do you live in Love? Do you follow and act from your heart or from your fears?

Take some time to think and write below about these four big subjects, as these subjects are really important for you to be happy and succeed in your life.

Faith

Do you have Faith?   YES ☐   NO ☐

If YES write something about it:

....

....

....

....

If you don't, why don't you?

....

....

....

....

....

....

....

Trust

- Do you have Trust?
- Do you trust that you will always be looked after?
- If you look back through your life have you not always been looked after?
- Or given what you've asked for?
- Our outer reflections are actually our inner reflections, so if you don't trust that all will be okay then maybe you don't fully trust yourself?
- If you fully trust yourself it does not matter where you end up because you will always trust yourself to do your best.
- Please write below whatever you want to write on this large subject of trust.

Hope

Do you have hope?   YES ☐   NO ☐

If you don't, why don't you?

....

....

....

....

....

Love

YES ☐   NO ☐

Do you act and follow from your heart?

Or do you act and follow from your mind or your fears?
Would you like to lead your life from your heart and the energy of love?

....

....

....

....

....

If yes, then make the promise below:

....

....

....

....

I .... promise
from this day forward
I will only act from my
heart and energy of love.
I will understand what my
ego, mind and fears are
telling me to do however
I choose to not follow
these fears or thoughts.
I choose to act out of
love.

Sign:
....

Manifesting Exercises

If you are ready for your purpose and dreams to come into your life quickly then follow the manifesting techniques on the next pages.

1. Visualising

For the next two weeks, spend every day visualising what it would be like if you were living your life purpose/goal/dreams.

2. Feeling

Whilst you are visualising I want you to actually feel the feeling you would have if you were living your life purpose. Feel the feeling for at least a couple of minutes. Do this three times per day and your dreams will manifest quickly.

3. Being grateful

Gratefulness always speeds up manifesting. I have included some gratefulness worksheets at the end. For the next two weeks, every morning or every evening write down five things you are grateful for.

4. Asking

Whatever it is you want, make sure you ask for it. Just say it out loud. Make the universe know that you want something and you are specifically asking for it.

5. Receiving

Be open to receiving. This could come in many forms, so if someone offers you help, kindly accept it. If you are offered an invitation, kindly accept it, and so forth.

6. Allowing

Allow your dreams to come into reality; don't let doubts or fears get in your way. if you start doubting your dreams and worrying it won't happen then that is exactly the outcome you will get.

7. Stay positive

That's why it is so important to stay positive. If you start to feel negative one day, put on your favourite song and dance your heart out. This will lift you up and bring you back to positivity. After you finish the dance, grab the gratitude worksheets and write down five things you are grateful for.

8. Take action

If you don't buy a lottery ticket then you will never win! Every single day take action on your dreams and watch them manifest. If you are confused about how to take action, then just sit in a quiet space, calm your mind, zone into yourself and just ask, **"Where do I start?"**

"What action can I take?" Sit, listen, and wait for the answer.

The more you zone into yourself and calm the mind, the more you will hear your own guidance and intuition. And don't forget to ask! This will be your biggest tool to success. If you still fully cannot hear your intuition and inner guidance, just keep practicing with the yin activities. One day you will hear it, and it will just be there. Guiding you.

On the next page you will complete an Intention Ritual. Within that ritual, you will write down your dreams from your heart. I want you to take the time and go down your list one by one, and I want you to feel how it will feel when you are doing the things you love. I want you to sit in a daydream, imagining you are doing the things you love, and feel the feeling you get when you are doing them. Take your time to do this for each dream you want to do and accomplish. Do not rush this stage; enjoy this stage. Take the time to visualise yourself doing it and visualise all the small details that go with this dream. Just sit in this dream and feel the feelings that will come when you're living it.

You are now going to read, write and sign the Intention Ritual below:

Intention Ritual

INTENTION RITUAL

Dear Higher Self,

Thank you for always being there for me and thank you for always loving me.

I .... make this promise to you, which is me.

I .... promise to love you, respect you and treat you with kindness.

I .... promise from this day forward I will take action on my dreams.

Write down what you want to become or what you want to accomplish within the next year.

1 ....

2 ....

3 ....

4 ....

5 ....

I am this person: (Write down five amazing things about yourself)

1 ....

2 ....

3 ....

4 ....

5 ....

Lots of Love,

Signature ....

Date ....

It's important that you trust you will accomplish your dreams and it is important to surrender to them, which means letting them go from your mind. When I say trust, that does not mean you sit and do nothing about your dreams and hope they come to you. It does not work like that. Now is the time that you have to put consistent action into your dreams. Decide what that means to you; whether it is two hours a week, every week without fail, or two hours a day every single day. This is your journey so jump in and start living it!

It is important that you surrender to the outcome. What does surrender mean? It means stop thinking actively about the end result. What will be will be; all you can do is put everyday actions towards your dreams to help turn them into reality. Just concentrate and enjoy each day of living your purpose. Your purpose is not the end result, it is the enjoyment of acting on your purpose every single day.

I hope this journal has taken you on a journey to yourself, to your heart and to your inner guidance. I hope you have implemented changes that will bring a brighter future for yourself and I know you will accomplish everything you want to. Just remember to stay with your heart energy.

I wish you the best of luck on your journey full of love, fulfilment and happiness.

Much love always,

Vayia Nafees x

be your spirit

YOUR
DAILY GRATITUDE
WORKSHEET

I am grateful for

I am grateful for

I am grateful for

I am grateful for

I am grateful for

I am grateful for

I am grateful for